HELP! SAID JED

story by Deborah Eaton
illustrations by Mike Reed

HARCOURT BRACE & COMPANY

Orlando Atlanta Austin Boston San Francisco Chicago Dallas New York
Toronto · London

Jed climbed up.

"Help!" said Jed.

Mom climbed up.
"Help!" said Jed.

Bret climbed up.
"Help!" said Jed.

Nell climbed up.
"Help!" said Jed.

"Thanks," said Jed.

"Now let's go," said Jed.
"Help!" they said.